Setting standards

A guide to achieving quality in the nursery

Ruth Andreski and Sarah Nicholls

A Nursery World Publication

Published by Nursery World Limited
© 1994

This book, which appeared in 12 monthly installments in Nursery World throughout 1993, is designed to give early years workers an ongoing opportunity to review the care their nursery provides. It has been written by former Advisory Teacher for Preschool and Nursery at Berkshire LEA, now a consultant and inspector of daycare nurseries, Ruth Andreski, and her colleague Sarah Nicholls, Lecturer and Early Years Co-ordinator at Reading University.

Acknowledgements

We would like to thank all those dedicated people who have welcomed us into their nurseries and playgroups. Their comments and suggestions gave us the impetus to develop this step-by-step guide.
Our thanks must also go to Pauline Hansford who has tirelessly deciphered our hand-written notes and transformed them into readable typescript.

First published 1995
Reprinted 1996

Dedication

To our long suffering families for their support and encouragement.

Published by Nursery World Limited, Unit A, The Schoolhouse Workshop, 51 Calthorpe Street, London WC1X 0HH.
All photographs by Johanna Mungo. Printed by Omega Print Ltd, Sidcup, Kent.
Our thanks to the Fielding Primary School, London Borough of Ealing.

CONTENTS

Provision for children under statutory school age is currently a widely discussed topic. For decades parents, politicians and professionals have argued the merits of providing nursery places for the children of parents who wish to give their sons and daughters educational opportunities before statutory school age. Issues concerning both the 'quantity' and 'quality' of nursery provision occur frequently in these debates.

This book, which originated as a series of articles published earlier in Nursery World, will help readers to identify 'quality education' in the nursery years and hopefully help them to become even greater advocates of high standards for young children.

The twelve chapters consider some of the main issues in early childhood care and education, looking not only at the curriculum but also focusing on the individual needs of children, including a section on gifted children. There are chapters on various aspects of play and children's learning, an area of education which is frequently undervalued in these days of emphasis on the 'basic skills'.

The importance of record keeping and observation are stressed and guidelines are given on how to develop effective strategies. Unlike many books in this field, it deals not only with the curriculum and practical aspects of children's development but also discusses the importance of developing management strategies within the nursery environment. Here again the authors have adopted a highly practical approach, emphasising the need for work in early childhood settings.

At present the traditional nursery school or class has come under attack from some quarters for failing to work effectively with parents. Those of us who have been in the field for many years know this to be untrue, but we are also aware that it is a highly sensitive area which needs full and frank discussion. The chapter on 'Working with parents' is a very clear and helpful one and should make a positive contribution to the field.

Fortunately this book, which was so well received by the readers of Nursery World when it was first published in installments, will now reach an even wider audience. All those working daily with children under statutory school age will find information and ideas to aid them in providing high quality care and education.

Audrey Curtis

4

Our work involves visiting a wide variety of childcare and education settings. In conversation with staff we became aware of frequent feelings of professional isolation and their need for more support and in-service training specifically geared to nursery work.

In producing this book we have taken into account the fact that training needs to be affordable and tailored to the varied settings that early years workers may be employed in, whilst still recognising the universality of children's needs at this vital stage of their development.

We hope that the framework of training we have provided will prove manageable and helpful in addressing crucial aspects of your practice. It has been designed to take into account the way children, adults, curriculum resources and facilities interrelate within any nursery.

You will decide which element of training you wish to begin with and the subsequent order you follow, as well as the time you devote to individual sections. However, we do strongly recommend that you begin with the first chapter 'Working as a team' since co-operation is the basis of all good nursery practice.

We believe that in today's climate, where appraisal and evaluation are high on everyone's agenda, our system of analysing practice should help individuals and teams to set realisable goals. These can then be translated into genuine improvements with consequent job satisfaction.

In following this programme of self-evaluation staff will feel much more confident when faced with inspection, either from OFSTED or the annual re-registration procedure undertaken by social services personnel.

Ruth Andreski and Sarah Nicholls

CHAPTER 1

Working as a team

Everybody in a nursery needs to feel that their contribution is essential to the team and is compatible with its overall philosophy. People might assume that this will be easier when starting a nursery from scratch, but this is not necessarily the case.

Normally, in a new establishment, the most senior person will be appointed first. This person needs a clear vision of the team that is to be built. Staff appointed later ought to be consulted about subsequent recruitment of other members so that a consensus is sought at each stage, but be aware of the dangers of 'cloning' and the advantages of employing 'new blood'.

'A good team will enjoy the advantage of having developed its guiding principles.'

A good team will enjoy the advantage of having developed its guiding principles. Potential staff members should have a chance to see these explicitly stated in writing as well as being carried out in practice. They can then join the organisation equipped with a knowledge of how it works and what is believed in, while existing team members know what kind of person they need to recruit.

Your team may well have members of staff who are differently qualified and trained. There may well be other adults involved with the nursery whose role is equally important, namely students, volunteers (often parents) and people on various training schemes or supervised work experience. Professional staff should have job descriptions which they have accepted. Involvement in the creation or modification of a job description will almost certainly generate enthusiasm and personal job satisfaction.

Careful thought must also be given to the precise nature of the role of students and volunteers within the team. In the case of the former, negotiation

may well have to take place between the training institution and the person responsible for the placements so that a consistent approach is assured. The aims and practices of the institution should be carefully explained (providing documentation wherever possible) as well as expectations of an individual's involvement. This will have the advantage of demonstrating good underlying organisation and management, as well as providing security and a sense of purpose for the helper.

The team needs to spend time discussing factors which are conducive to good relationships, promote co-operation and obviate or resolve possible conflict. Making time to consider relationships and team building within the work setting should come before anything else, since the success of essential issues like organisation and the curriculum often depends on the adults who work on them – on their happiness, enthusiasm and co-operation. No-one can afford to waste the human effort which inevitably occurs when people feel misunderstood, insecure, or put upon. Furthermore, the ethos and atmosphere generated by a happy staff will influence the emotional climate in which the children are being cared for. Time spent considering relationships implicitly states that we value them, and, since everybody will be involved, we are also demonstrating our commitment to a collegiate approach to management particularly appropriate in a child education or childcare setting.

'The ethos and atmosphere generated by a happy staff will influence the emotional climate in which the children are being cared for.'

The very act of sitting down and talking about these suggested issues will help people to get to know each other in a way that a pre-organised daily routine can never permit. Before beginning a discussion session, however, it must be remembered that some people, often the more junior members or the least qualified and experienced, may feel reluctant to state their views. Skill and sensitivity is required to involve them. It is helpful to ask people to arrive at meetings with a note pad, pen and diary. Thoughts already set down on paper tend to be clearer and more easily stated, so it is important to have agendas for meetings. It is surprising how having a few notes will give confidence to even the most timid people. Moreover, the chairperson can indicate at the beginning of the exercise that everyone's views will be considered.

An excellent ice-breaker is to ask everyone to jot down what it is that they feel most strongly about in the whole world. People are usually happy to expound on their pet hobby horse! Once everybody has had a say in this exercise – which is essentially rather fun – it should not be too difficult for them to contribute on more focused matters.

'We must express our own opinions honestly and freely.'

1. **Begin by focusing on recent successes. To what extent have they been the result of colleagues co-operating well together?**
2. **If you had to produce a 'Team Manifesto' would you all agree that the following principles would be included?**
    - We should all be ourselves and not play a part we feel others would like.
    - We must express our own opinions honestly and freely.
    - We must offer ideas we have for improvements in the way we work together.
    - Team members should be able to say if something is wrong and not 'bottle up' feelings.
    - We all recognise that everybody makes mistakes, so team members should admit an error and make every effort to put it right.
    - If mistakes have been made we should all be prepared to help put them right if it proves to be necessary.
    - Team members should feel free to disagree, on the understanding that this does not imply personal animosity against the person with whom they disagree.

- We should all try to be tolerant, recognising each other's right to hold different opinions and the value of diversity in the team.
- We try to support one another by sharing the work fairly, keeping our word and completing tasks on time.

Finally, are there any misunderstandings or mistakes which have occurred in the team which could have been avoided had we all been really committed to the contents of the above manifesto?

3. You can use the following case studies to promote discussion on team relationships.

SONIA is a team member who is coming to the end of her career. She complains of back pains and headaches which mean that she cannot be expected to do 'too much'. Others are finding that she increasingly asks them to support her.

BRENDA claims to love her work. She has asked for a key to the building so that she can come in early, at about 7.40am. She avoids coffee breaks and lunch times saying she does not know how people find time for them. Immediately after the afternoon session she makes a quick cup of tea before scurrying off to her room – giving disapproving looks to anyone who may be 'having a chat'. She remains hard at work until at least 6.30pm every evening and has been known to stay until 9.30pm. She also likes to come in every other Saturday. She makes sure that parents know about her efforts and tells them in such a way that she implies that they cannot possibly be covering all that needs to be done and may be letting their children down.

'Brenda claims to love her work. She has asked for a key so that she can come in early.'

SUSAN is a young nursery nurse. She has a real gift for storytelling and has a plethora of ideas to enhance her performance. Children really enjoy her session and sit transfixed. The senior member of staff with whom she works finds this rather threatening and has recently been finding reasons why Susan should tidy-up while she takes the story sessions instead.

ELAINE avoids disagreements and conflict at all times. She has become adept at agreeing with everything others say. She is intuitive enough to guess fairly successfully what people would like to hear and then proceeds to say it. On the occasions when she is not sure what to say, she uses 'testers' which she does not have to own. In this way she can pursue the conversations armed with the knowledge her listeners have provided through their reactions.

4. **Discuss issues concerning temporary team members (volunteers, students). Care must be given to the precise nature of the role of students and volunteers within the establishment. It saves a lot of time, effort and possible misunderstanding if the team devises a brief handout on commonly-occurring nursery activities which will:**

   a) Explain the adult role.

   b) List necessary resources.

   c) Encourage good organisation.

   d) Cause them to think about the educational potential.

'Care must be given to the precise nature of the role of students and volunteers.'

Situations in which volunteers and students are frequently engaged in include:

1. A visit.

2. Cooking with a group.

3. Participating in a game.

4. Participating in a creative activity.

5. Participating in imaginative play.

6. Sharing books with children.

7. Outdoor activities eg gardening.

8. Observing natural phenomena like rainbows, or bird feeding.

9. Making and mending.

10. Demonstrating a skill, talent, or an aspect of a special personal interest.

We offer the following format as an example so that you can develop other exercises applicable to your situation.

COOKING WITH A GROUP

A: The adult role

1. Make a list of participating children.

2. Note any special needs factors which have to be taken into account, eg the diabetic child who shouldn't eat the mixture!

3. Think about safety factors – hygiene, cooking hazards, burning, sharp instruments, etc.

4. As with everything else, be sure the children do the work and encourage them to talk about the task.

B: Necessary resources

1. What are you cooking?

2. Have you the necessary utensils, ingredients and recipe?

3. Do you know where the equipment is kept?

4. Do you know how the cooker works?

5. If necessary, have you been given the money to purchase the ingredients?

C: The organisation

1. Children should be dressed for the task and wash their hands.

2. Explain what you are going to do.

3. Make sure all children can see, hear and participate.

4. Everybody should clear up!

D: Development and outcomes

1: Cooking teaches much about maths – it helps the children to count, weigh, measure, share and sort.

2. It also helps with science – raising issues of colour change, use of senses and predicting outcomes.

3. To help with English, let children help you read the recipe, then discuss the ingredients – where they come from, the children's likes, dislikes, shopping, etc, to help increase their vocabulary.

CHAPTER 2

Working with parents

'Parents can significantly influence their children's learning but this potential contribution needs to be fully recognised and acknowledged.'
(Starting with Quality, DES, 1990.)

In this second chapter, we examine ways in which early years workers can make parents feel part of the nursery community.

TALKING ABOUT THE IMPORTANCE OF PARENTS

Here the team is asked to examine itself in relation to the neighbourhood it serves.

'The team is asked to examine itself in relation to the neighbourhood it serves.'

1. **Do we attempt to get to know parents before their children come to us? Ways of achieving this are:**
    *   Instigating careful discussions at registration time.
    *   Establishing pre-entry visits.
    *   Making close contact with other childcare providers.
    *   Starting a parents' group with occasional meetings for parents before their children enter the nursery.
    *   Making home visits.

2. **Do we, as early years workers, encourage parents to play an active part in their children's education? How do we let them know how they can achieve this:**
    *   In the home?
    *   With us?

3. **Are parent helpers given a clear indication of what they have to do and why they are doing it?**
   - Have we made them aware of our philosophy, aims and objectives?
   - How have we done this?
   - Are they helped to see the relationship between the practice and fruition of aims?
   - Are there ample opportunities for informal discussions on a regular basis?
   - Should we have regular meetings with individual parents on a formal basis?
   - Are we always sensitive to the needs of parents, and able to 'pick up' on anxieties and smooth out trouble before it really begins?

'Should we have regular meetings with individual parents on a formal basis?'

4. **Are all letters and notices for parents:**
   - Succinct?
   - Well laid out?
   - Grammatically correct?
   - Free of spelling mistakes? The latter gives a very bad impression of us as educators.

5. **Do we send out too many letters? Can they sometimes be replaced by:**
   - A notice on the board?
   - A verbal message?

6. **Are there occasions when the parent body is encouraged:**
   - To socialise?
   - To fundraise?
   - To share in celebrations?

- To join a making and mending workshop?

7. Is there a medium through which parents can express their views?

8. Are the parents involved in the compilation of their children's records?

PARTNERSHIP: A DISCUSSION SESSION

Examine, as a team, how you can best try to meet the needs of the following parents:

MS A: 'I know it's silly but I just went home and cried when I took Ian to the nursery – I even found myself resenting the staff.'

MS B: 'If I spoke the real honest truth, I must say that I felt a sense of liberation – you know, peace at last to do what I wanted to do... it's a hell of a sacrifice having a kid. I wouldn't be without her now, but I guess I'm not really the maternal type.'

'I know it's silly
but I just went
home and
cried when I
took Ian to the
nursery.'

MR E: 'I'm glad Mark is going to have some feminine influence in his life now he's started with you. I had to give up work to look after the kids when my wife left me. I'd quite like to offer my services but it's difficult for a bloke among all those mothers.'

MS F: 'I wish the place could take her full-time, then I could look for a decent job, 'cause it's hard managing on my own and I get lonely in the flat.'

GLENDA: 'My childminder is excellent. She collects Victoria from nursery and sometimes keeps her when I'm late home after meetings – but I wish I had time to talk to the staff and see what Victoria is doing for myself.'

HAMID: 'It's necessary for Jawaid to learn good English before school. My wife's English is not good – she is busy looking after the other children.'

IAN AND RUTH: 'We've had a lot of help from Mrs Jones, the preschool counsellor. We're so anxious that Jeremy learns to mix with the other children and in spite of all his problems, we do so hope he'll go on to normal school.'

JANE: 'My boyfriend says Tracy's ever so naughty and it's time she learned to behave herself. She still wets the bed and she's nearly four.'

DEVELOPING A POSITIVE NEIGHBOURHOOD IMAGE

- Is the garden attractive and inviting? Could it be improved? Is it regularly checked for safety, is it free of litter and graffiti?
- Is the 'Way In' clearly indicated to visitors?
- Is the lobby, entrance or place where parents and visitors wait, tidily arranged?
- Is the notice board looking fresh and up-to-date, with sections for managing committees, governors, staffing and parent-to-parent meetings?
- Has the staff group given time and thought to the publication of the 'Welcome booklet'? Does it include sections on management committees, governors, staffing, hours, dress, broad aims, links with the community, the curriculum, how parents can help, drinks and snacks, health issues, records, festivals, parent/educator discussions, admissions policy and so on?
- What criteria should we have in mind when choosing our own working clothes? Do clothes matter?
- What kind of non-verbal messages are we conveying to visitors – are they friendly or frantic?
- What of the nursery display? This should not be window dressing but reflect the children's work, invite curiosity and appeal to the senses. The main purpose of a display is to educate, not decorate. Does your display satisfy these criteria? Are your colour schemes well chosen?
- Are your displays varied? Do they include technology, mathematics, art,

'What kind of non-verbal messages are we conveying to visitors?'

15

the natural and living world, the environment and different materials?

- Do we go out of our way to establish and maintain links with other agencies?
- Do we make ourselves available to give talks, or to join in discussions or activities with those groups concerned with the education of young children?
- Do we put ourselves forward to represent our establishment in the community in carnivals, exhibitions and other events?
- When visitors look at the children they are likely to ask: Are they happy? Are they busy? Are they learning? Are they showing consideration for one another? Do the children relate happily to the adults?

'Those who receive the children stand to gain a lot from visiting parents in the home.'

HOME VISITS

Those who receive the children stand to gain a lot from visiting parents in the home. Parents almost invariably welcome this meeting, particularly those for whom education was not the happiest of experiences.

A home visit provides an opportunity to:

- Establish the notion of partnership with parents.
- Talk about your aims and those of the organisation.
- Persuade parents of the value of shared record-keeping procedures as a means of charting and guiding their child's progress.
- Listen to any concerns that the parents may have.
- See the child in his formative setting.
- Persuade them that you are people in whom they can have complete confidence.

Consider the following when establishing your own home visiting policy:

- How will you word your statement on home visits in your brochure/ 'Welcome booklet'?
- How will you design a friendly notification card to be sent to parents when a visit is imminent?

- Should you suggest the date or leave that to the parents?
- How many of you will carry out the visit?
- Have you worked out strategies for possible embarrassing or difficult encounters? Remember these visits may be the most difficult but ultimately the most important for the child.

What will you take?

- A photograph album depicting staff and children engaged in normal activities as well as enjoying special occasions.
- Sample child records.
- A toy, game or picture book to share with the child.

Have you worked out your philosophy of preschool education and can you defend the value of play to a sceptical adult? If parents ask what they can do to help, have you got your answers ready? Finally, do you see this as an excellent time to begin the child's records with parental observations?

CHAPTER 3

The nursery environment

Within the nursery environment there is an ongoing framework that should be the backbone of any good educational setting for under fives. This needs to be defined before one can examine the use that can be made of the provision. Once this has been identified, the organisation of materials and time must also be given consideration. Finally a review needs to be carried out to ensure that a balanced curriculum is being provided which will inevitably include appropriate aspects of the national curriculum.

'A review needs to be carried out to ensure that a balanced curriculum is being provided.'

THE BASIC PROVISION

Sand – wet and dry.

Water.

Home area.

Book corner.

Art activities – 2D.

Craft activities – 3D.

Large construction blocks.

Small construction materials.

Table top activities – small world artifacts, jigsaw puzzles etc.

Music area.

Cooking facilities/Milk kitchen.

Live animals and plants.

Investigative area.

Space and time for expansive physical activities – PE, drama, movement.

Quiet area/baby sleep-room.

Well-equipped outside area/Use of outside environment.

Staff room/toilet.

Toilets/washroom/laundry.

1: Examine your environment and ask yourself:

- Do we have all of these?
- If not, why not?
- How are these areas organised?
- How might these areas be developed to realise their maximum potential?

When examining the organisation of your materials you will have to ask the following questions:

Does the room look organised, clean, bright and inviting?

Are the dangerous items clearly labelled, correctly stored and out of children's reach?

Are the resources easily accessible and clearly labelled for children and adults?

Is the work area used effectively?

Consider whether all the following areas are being exploited to the full:

> Wet area.
>
> Dry area.
>
> Passageways.
>
> Quiet area.
>
> Open area.
>
> Noisy area.

Are the resources required for each area stored nearby?

Is the outside environment an integral part of the children's learning?

'Does the room look organised, clean, bright and inviting?'

2: Plans

Draw a floor plan of the nursery. Could you organise the basic provision within the areas more effectively? Bear in mind:

> Access/emergency exits.

Movement pathways.

Type of flooring.

Storage.

Safety.

The needs of each activity.

Appropriate activities existing in proximity to each other.

'Are books exchanged frequently enough to introduce variety and freshness?'

3: The book corner

We have looked at the book corner in detail but suggest that you look in equal detail at all other areas.

Look critically at the book corner. Has it gradually become rather sad looking and uninviting? Do the adults actually spend time there? Their involvement gives important messages to children about books. Whether revamping or setting up a new book corner you need to ask:

- Is the level or height of the display right for young children's use?
- Is the area attractive, quiet and comfortable?
- Is the type of lighting appropriate – is it natural or artificial?
- Can books be easily withdrawn from the shelf/box/display case?
- Has the actual quality of the books been looked at?
- Are there enough books?
- Is the selection subject to the list here entitled 'Criteria for book selection'?
- Are books exchanged frequently enough to introduce variety and freshness?
- Are storytellers invited in? Local libraries can be helpful here, as well as talented parents and neighbours.

Criteria for book selection:

It is obviously important that we select books for children with great care. For some it may be their first introduction to the magical world of literature and the possibility that books hold for extending experience of the natural world, as well

as answering many of their questions and satisfying emotional needs.

You need to bear the following factors in mind:

- The use of language and style involving familiarity, while also offering sufficient challenge through new vocabulary.
- The inclusion of poetry as well as prose.
- The quality of illustration and photographs.
- The durability of binding and pages.
- The price: some books are excellent value for money or you can buy others cheaply at book sales.
- The inclusion of some books which are suitable for small or even large group work.
- A balance in literature between the traditional and the 'latest thing'.
- Books should offer positive messages on equality of both race and gender.
- Information books should be available to support the themes you undertake with the children.
- There should be a balance between fantasy and fact.

'Information books should be able to support the themes you undertake with the children.'

4. Time

When you have looked at the physical organisation of the nursery environment you need to look at the organisation of time.

- How long is the session?
- How is the session divided?
- If it is not divided, why not?

Put yourself in the children's shoes – does this give you time to experience a variety of activities each day? Would you get frustrated by lack of activities?

Are all the children grouped appropriately according to their age and stage of development? Are the rest or sleep times meeting individual children's needs?

Remember, you need to provide a working and workable structure in which the children and adults can live, learn and grow, but your structure must not become a straitjacket. Children need the freedom to explore and learn from their environment. Many children's lives have become constrained by dangers associated with our modern lifestyle – whether they are road, human or environmental dangers. We have the responsibility to put back the freedom and enjoyment of life for our children and thus allow them to explore and grow through their experiences.

'Children need the freedom to explore and learn from their environment.'

CURRICULUM AUDIT

To ensure that your curriculum is broad and balanced (and incidentally meeting many of the targets of the national curriculum!) it will be necessary to undertake an 'audit' of the curriculum you are providing.

The social area of learning

Do you encourage children in the various activities on offer in the nursery?

Do you help them to acquire skills and thereby develop their confidence?

Do you, through example, opportunity and discussion enable children to learn to respect others and be able to co-operate with them?

Do staff set a framework for appropriate behaviour in the different situations that the nursery offers?

Does the ethos you have created enable children to relate happily to adults as well as to each other?

The linguistic area of learning and experience

Are staff aware of the supreme importance of discussion in developing children's language competence?

Do you make speaking and listening a part of all the activities you offer?

Are a wide variety of stories, poems, rhymes and songs presented and children encouraged to commit some of these to memory?

Does your book corner and storytelling time feature prominently in the nursery curriculum?

Do you help children learn to love books and use them appropriately?

Do you encourage children to understand that print conveys meaning?

Do adults share books with them?

Do you label their work, displays and resources and draw their attention to print within the environment?

Are opportunities given for children to make marks on paper, drawing, scribbling and eventually possibly learning to write some letters accurately?

Do your children have opportunities to convey messages?

Are staff aware of their role as models for children's language?

Is adequate consideration given to the quality of explanations and instructions offered?

The physical area of learning

Gross Motor

Do opportunities exist within your nursery for children to run, jump, climb, balance and use a variety of small apparatus for throwing, catching, rolling, riding on, pushing, pulling etc?

Is time made for specific mime and movement sessions?

Fine motor

Do you organise your nursery so that children have an opportunity to use a wide range of tools and equipment and handle many kinds of material?

The mathematical area of experience

Do you offer an extensive range of items thus enabling your children to sort and classify, match, order and count?

Are there opportunities for children to handle and discuss a range of two and three dimensional shapes?

Are staff helping children to acquire the language of comparison, eg taller than/shorter than, lighter than/heavier than, larger/smaller than?

Are children being helped to use the language of spatial relationships – such words as 'on', 'under', 'above', 'below', 'turn over' and 'turn round' which should become part of their vocabulary in the activities they pursue.

The scientific and technological area of learning

Do opportunities abound for children to observe phenomena, materials and things from the natural world at first hand, using their senses?

Are they encouraged to describe and discuss what they see and to notice similarities and differences?

Do you encourage children to question why things happen and say how they think things work?

Do you present simple experiments, carefully supervised, to incorporate the scientific method which involves observation, prediction, experimentation and communicating a conclusion, eg a) drying the washing in different situations, b) freezing water, then melting the ice in various places.

Do you provide children with the freedom to make things?

Are there ample opportunities to solve the many problems which present themselves?

Are you providing a wide range of tools and materials from which the children can choose to work?

Do you present collections of items from the 'man-made' world eg different spoons, brushes or footwear so that children can discuss what materials such things are made of and why?

Within the boundaries of safety and under close supervision do you encourage children to use new technology, tape recorders, videos – even the computer, if you are lucky enough to have one? Do they talk about experiences with such things?

The aesthetic and creative area of experience

Do the staff plan for children to express themselves in a wide variety of ways, including: drawing, collage, painting, modelling in malleable materials such as clay and dough; making models with waste materials, construction kits and blocks; making an environment in which they can play, eg a space rocket or a boat? Are there opportunities for them to express themselves in role play, drama/mime, dance and music? Do they listen to music?

Do children have simple techniques demonstrated to them and are they given ample opportunities to practice and perfect them?

CHAPTER 4

Working outside

Outdoor activities provide a starting point for helping a child come to terms with his environment and the extended community.

The garden – if there is one – should be fully used by children. This is of particular importance in urban areas where they frequently lack the opportunity to exercise their right of freedom to enjoy space, fresh air and an opportunity to interact with nature. Children should have free access to both outside and inside environments. Sometimes people need to be reminded that education is just as likely to occur outside as well as inside – it is not a four walls phenomenon!

Those working with young children need to ask themselves if what they think of as an inside activity could not be carried out equally well outside – painting, construction, sand and water play, story time, and so on.

The way children play when allowed to interact with the outside world provides pointers to what we should provide for them in the nursery garden:

They run, jump and climb.

They excavate.

They play with water.

They play with mud.

They collect objects like pebbles, shells, nuts, fruits.

They like to hide.

They roll down slopes.

They make camps in secret places.

They step on stones or lines, or cross sections of logs.

They push and pull vehicles.

They grow things and harvest them.

They look at prevailing flora and fauna.

Above all, perhaps, the garden provides those who cultivate it with a sense of achievement and to make sure it does we need to address the following questions:

- Do you have a place where children can dig in addition to normal sand play?
- Do you have good collections of interesting natural objects?
- Have you got a sloped area – if not, can you create one?
- Do you have stepping games – stones, logs, tiles?
- Do you have equipment or facilities for climbing?
- Is there a 'natural' place to hide?
- Do you have materials for children to make camps, such as sheets, rugs, blankets, frameworks for draping over?
- Do your vehicles encourage individual and co-operative use, and can they be pulled and pushed?
- Is there a flat area for children to use wheeled vehicles?
- Is there an area in the outside environment where children can actually garden and harvest their products?
- Have you grown, harvested and prepared the following:
  beans
  potatoes

'Do you think
of the outdoor
dimensions
when you are
planning the
curriculum.'

tomatoes

pumpkins

raspberries

apples

herbs

sunflowers?

To ensure variety, consider:

evergreen and deciduous plants

flowering shrubs

scented shrubs

vegetables and fruit

a herb garden

a compost-making facility.

Have you contacted parents to help, ie through donating plants and cuttings?

Have you considered using planted tubs if necessary?

Do you have a polythene-covered plant propagator?

Do you have child-sized gardening tools?

– an outside tap and hose?

– wheelbarrows?

– watering cans?

Have you considered attracting animals to your garden by installing:

A bird table.

A wild area.

Plants to attract butterflies and other insects,

ie buddleia, nasturtiums.

Cover for wood-lice, snails.

Wet land habitats – pond and marshy ground?

Where do you store the equipment which is used for outdoor activities?

Is it easily accessible?

Do you think of the outdoor dimensions when you are planning the curriculum?

Are you promoting science, English, maths, geography, RE and technology through activities in the garden?

Are you fully recognising the garden as a valuable resource for integrating different aspects of children's development?

THE OUTSIDE ENVIRONMENT – OPPORTUNITIES FOR DEVELOPMENT

SOCIAL AND MORAL

There are plenty of social opportunities here for sharing, taking turns and co-operation. Opportunities often arise for encouraging empathy with, and to develop a sense of personal responsibility for, other children, plants and animals. Children can also be encouraged to develop a sense of wonder at the marvels of the natural world – growth, the weather, colour, form and pattern.

Ask yourself these questions:

Do you plan walks for a purpose which is readily understood by the children and which can provide excellent opportunities for language development through experiences and discussion, for example:

To buy goods?

To post letters and/or parcels?

To look for print in the environment?

To visit a particular public building, eg place of worship, nursery, library?

To see somebody at work?

To consider road safety?

To collect natural objects?

To help children become aware of different types of building to consider what they are used for?

To see different kinds of transport using the road?

To look at the different things people are doing?

To look at natural phenomena or particular plants or animals?

To listen to the sounds which abound in the locality?

Do you use this exploration of the locality to encourage children to express their

'Do you plan walks for a purpose which is readily understood by the children?'

likes and dislikes about its features?

Do you encourage a sense of stewardship through pointing out the importance of the correct disposal of litter into bins and draw children's attention to public activities like planting and tending parks and gardens, caring for animals, etc?

Do you use the work outside to draw children's attention to the use of directions and spatial concepts like:

'Turn round the corner.'

'Cross over the road.'

'Go under or over the bridge.'

EMOTIONAL

The wider world can seem daunting to insecure children. Are you aware of individuals who need encouragement to develop self-confidence and a sense of security?

PHYSICAL

Equipment and facilities need to be available to encourage motor development. Do not forget that many motor skills can also be exercised outside.

INTELLECTUAL

The natural environment, the additions made to it and the adult's role in encouraging exploration and discovery is vital.

Essential points to remember

What is the quality of interaction between adults and children? Be aware of body language and facial expressions. Are you talking about and sharing the experiences with the children?

Whether or not you have a garden – and you are clearly at an advantage if you do – there are aspects of children's education which need to be catered for outside the confines of the premises and in the wider environment. It is particularly important that children in full daycare should experience activities normally undertaken by parents with their children. These activities help them to

'It is particularly important that children in full daycare should experience activities normally undertaken by parents with their children.'

make more sense of their environment and the work done by those in it.

Use your local community workers if you can – sometimes children from a local secondary school are happy to be given work experience in nurseries – speak to the head teacher.

Finally, find out from the library about any local environmental groups which could provide help and information. It is well worth subscribing to an organisation if necessary. Don't forget the advantage of ceremonies – they make excellent vehicles for language development in young children, they promote social harmony and raise the profile of what you are trying to do. If you hold a tree-planting ceremony or a harvest festival, the local media can be asked to cover it which gives you an immediate platform from which to tell the world about the importance of your work as educators.

CHAPTER 5

Purposeful play

Many educators have remarked, with regret, that the life of the modern child is considerably constrained. The environment beyond the garden is seen by many parents to be beset by danger – child molesters and environmental hazards of various kinds. Although instant and sensational media coverage may well exaggerate the danger, parents often feel forced to curtail their children's freedom much more than was the case in previous generations.

A second form of constraint on the natural inclinations of young children is the nature of many modern homes, which are often fitted with a wealth of gadgets. Their style and decor may suit the adult, but they are incompatible with a young child's need to be physically active, experiment with all kinds of materials, make things and pursue improvised construction for imaginative play. All too often their experience is vicarious; it is lived through the television or computer screen. Families, too, are smaller and often separated by distance, so the range of playmates for the under fives is restricted for much of the time. This situation places considerable responsibility on preschool workers to provide a setting for learning which will foster and sustain a child's innate curiosity.

In Chapter 3 ('The nursery environment'), we encouraged you to examine your resources and organisation – a nursery can become dull and lacklustre unless the adults provide carefully thought out additions and use all their skills to maximise the potential that the environment has to offer. So, if we are to stimulate and satisfy curiosity, our efforts must lie in considering very carefully those extra things that we provide.

There is a sense in which there needs to be a 'surprise' every day – a special moment or opportunity – something new to look at, handle or discuss. Young children view the world with fresh eyes and it is easy to forget that what may be mundane for adults is full of possibilities for a child. Surprises concentrate the mind, enabling children to extend their understanding of the world through interaction with the materials or events or beings that are presented – extending their range of skills, concepts and knowledge.

There is a three-pronged involvement in the development of exploratory and purposeful play:

1. Opportunity.
2. Additions made to the basic provision which excite and renew interest – these will include discussion and questioning.
3. Satisfying their curiosity once this has been aroused, whereby the child engages with the activity in hand and learns through this engagement.

'The adult role in stimulating exploratory and purposeful play is an interesting one.'

So where do we begin? How do we categorise the additions we wish to make to the basic provision already in place? We can begin with the following groups which can be examined in detail later: people, collections, natural phenomena, interactive displays.

The adult role in stimulating exploratory and purposeful play is an interesting one. There are three possibilities here and we need to consider their implications. OPTION A: Set out the learning environment and then stand back. OPTION B: Set out the learning environment and then direct children in its use. OPTION C: Set out the learning environment and move in and out of the situation at times deemed appropriate.

OPTION A

This may lead to early boredom, possible frustration and a failure to maximise learning potential.

OPTION B

Here the child may well lack the necessary intrinsic motivation to undertake the tasks an adult is directing him to do. He may, as a consequence of this system, fail to develop initiative. Moreover, the task may not match the child's level of development and therefore fail in its purpose to educate him.

OPTION C

This seems to be a much more satisfactory position for the adult to adopt, but how will we know when to intervene and when to give children the time and space to explore their own ideas, and come into contact with objects and events with a sense of discovery? This can only be learned through careful observation.

NURTURING CURIOSITY

What are we providing to create opportunities for the development of curiosity? What are our aims and objectives in providing the particular items we have chosen?

What is our role in:
 - presentation
 - engagement
 - follow up
 - end result (if any)?

If we return to the suggested additions to our normal provision, we can ask ourselves questions which, through answering them, will reveal the richness of the extra dimensions of learning which we have made available to children.

PEOPLE AS A RESOURCE

Children invariably react to visitors with curiosity and the potential of the latter to develop their language and concentration through involvement and interest is undeniable.

Do you invite people into the nursery:
With interesting collections of things to show?

Skills and crafts to demonstrate?

Special jobs to talk about eg a policeman, a nurse or a hairdresser?

Parents with newborn babies to bath and to dress?

People with animals, such as a blind person with a guide dog, a farmer with a lamb or calf?

Someone with musical talent to share?

Those who can show facets of another culture, bringing clothes, artifacts, food or information about ceremonies with them?

People who can relate stories and experiences from the past?

COLLECTIONS TO EXPLORE

Collections invite exploration, manipulation, questions and generate discussion. Do you set up displays such as:

Lenses to look through.

Objects with which to make sounds, textures, scents and tastes.

Shapes with which to construct mechanical artifacts and toys.

An environment (perhaps outside) which the child can enter and explore from many angles? This may take the form of a garden where children have grown various plants.

Do not forget that handling and discussing artifacts from the past forms an important part of children's historical understanding.

'Collections invite exploration, manipulation, questions and generate discussion.'

LOOKING AT NATURAL PHENOMENA

It becomes increasingly important that we foster children's sense of wonder about and respect for the natural world. We need to encourage a sense of stewardship towards the natural environment in each child in our care.

Do you create displays to accomplish this aim?

Some examples you might include in a display are:

'Do you encourage children to look at works of art?'

> Grasses.
>
> Shells.
>
> Leaves.
>
> Flowers and roots.
>
> The growth of seeds.
>
> Rocks and minerals.
>
> Bark and twigs.
>
> A bird table in the nursery.
>
> Garden.
>
> An aquarium/vivarium.
>
> Small pets.
>
> Mini-beasts.
>
> The hatching of eggs – insect or bird.

Do you draw the children's attention to the weather?

Do you encourage children to look at works of art by regularly featuring them as part of your decor, for example: collages, paintings, carvings, weaving and textiles, ceramics, tools and artifacts with which the artist works, metal-ware and so on?

Do you consider colour, texture and variety of materials when you are purchasing new and essential equipment and furniture for the nursery, such as:

> The waste paper bin.
>
> The door mat.
>
> Curtaining.
>
> Table cloths.

Library cushions.

Cooking utensils.

Home corner furnishing?

We need to try to be on our guard against the temptation to purchase too much primary coloured plastic material to fill the nursery, just because it is easily available, clinically hygienic and cheap.

CREATING INTERACTIVE DISPLAYS

It is important that children should use, discuss and evaluate everyday objects. We need to encourage them to consider the object in relation to its function and recognise that it was designed and made to solve a problem. Children need to be encouraged to evaluate objects in terms of form and function.

Do you create displays of man-made objects like:

spoons

brushes

cups

teapots?

Do you discuss these objects with children asking questions like:

'What is it made of?'

'What is it for?'

'Does it do its job well?'

'Do you like it?'

'Which one do you like best?'

Do you encourage children's lateral thinking in relation to man-made objects?

It is through challenging assumptions that technological innovation takes place. For example, everybody believed that chairs had to be sat upon until somebody came up with the idea of kneeling on one and leaning forwards instead of backwards. Such chairs are said by some to be extremely comfortable!

CHAPTER 6

Imaginative and creative play

The possession of imagination is one of our greatest gifts as human beings. It is closely linked with creativity – indeed, creativity is the tangible expression of our imagination.

What are we looking at in terms of imagination and creativity? Opportunities can easily be provided for children through art, craft, design and some aspects of technology, music, dance and drama. All these areas promote development of imagination and creativity through the use of media and materials. We must provide a working environment that allows free play and enables children to make choices. Many manifestations of the imagination require the development of skills to enable children to explore their environment, otherwise their creativity and imagination will be limited.

We need to guard against always providing children with toys and equipment which, by their very sophistication and authenticity, require no use of imagination on the child's part. The child sitting in a box whose mind transforms it into a car will not only have to imagine that it is a car, but may be prompted to improvise, problem-solve and create in order to make the box look and behave more like a car.

How do we assess what we provide? Use the following headings to examine what the nursery provides.

DRAWING

Materials and space for drawing should always be available. Drawings must be the children's own and attempts by adults to impose ideas either through the provision of templates or giving them adult drawings to copy should be resisted.

Such examples tend to sap children's confidence and willingness to try, or, moreover, could foster stereotyped ideas of images.

WORKING WITH COLOUR

Children should be encouraged to paint on different coloured backgrounds and on paper of different shapes. They should also experience working on table tops and on easels. They should have the opportunity to use a wide range of colours and be encouraged to mix these to increase the range and make new ones.

Do you encourage children to:

Paint on different backgrounds, offering variety of colour, texture and material (though usually this will be paper)?

Work on different shaped backgrounds?

Experience painting both on table tops and a slanted easel?

Work with a wide range of colours, as well as black and white?

Experiment with mixing paints to achieve various shades and colours?

Use pastels, chalks, wax crayons and coloured pencils?

Try tie-and-dye techniques?

Apply colour using fingers, sponges, various brushes, straws to blow paint and items for printing such as string, cork, potato, leaves?

'A variety of items to choose from will give children the pleasure of deciding on appropriate colour, shape and texture.'

COLLAGE

This is a rewarding activity for children, as well as teaching them how to apply glue and cut and stick things properly. A variety of items to choose from will give children the pleasure of deciding on appropriate colour, shape and texture for the particular purpose. This exercise will also give them the opportunity to handle such materials as seeds, wood shavings, fabric, metal, string and different kinds of papers and plastic.

DESIGNING AND MAKING

Children should be given opportunities to make things for a purpose using their own designs. To enable this to happen you need to structure situations where a need is perceived and respond to the children's prompting. The range of things they can design is wide, but adults need to be aware of the appropriateness of the situation for the age group and avoid, at all costs, any tendency to impose a standard design for all the children to copy. Even more important is the need for adults to resist actually making the object themselves while pretending that the children did it! In any nursery brochure the importance of developing children's creativity should be stressed.

Think about whether you facilitate designing and making through:

- Encouraging children to want to make things.
- Helping children develop necessary skills through giving them opportunities for sewing, cutting, stitching, nailing and connecting.
- Providing a wide range of materials with different physical properties including clay, fabric, paper, metal, wood, food, card, plastic materials.
- Promoting the idea of settings for imaginative play, asking children what

'Avoid, at all costs, any tendency to impose a standard design for all the children to copy.'

they would like to do. Their suggestions might include:

A spaceship.

A sailing boat.

A hospital or dental surgery.

A garden centre.

Various shops or an office.

Rooms in a house.

- Encouraging them to make things which allow movement like:

Puppets.

Pop-up people.

Mobiles.

Models.

- Promoting discussion in the planning, making and evaluating of what they produce.

- Asking children to devise ways of carrying out activities, thinking about the sub-tasks in the process, like:
Cooking.
Bathing a baby.
Planting seeds.
Doing the washing.

MOVEMENT AND DRAMA

Both are an excellent means of expression, enabling children to develop an awareness of their own bodies and potential. Opportunities for movement and drama also promote social development through co-operation and self-confidence. Care must be taken to distinguish between performing plays and educational drama, where adults encourage children to experience all the roles.

Consider whether you:

- Enable children to express stories through acting out important aspects together. This is often most enjoyable when the adults participate.
- Plan your movement sessions to encourage bodily awareness.
- Build in concepts like fast/slow, tall/short, stretch/curl, follow/lead.
- Use movement sessions as a time to explore types of movement like twist, run, stop, stretch, shrink, creep, go under, go over, go though, go round.
- Enhance the quality of movement/drama through appropriate sound inspiration and make sure dressing up clothes and props are always available.
- Enable drama to be expressed through a variety of puppets.
- Enable children to work imaginatively with 'small world' toys. Do you have a sufficient variety of these?
- Encourage the development of symbolism through 'small world' representational toys or understood and agreed substitutions, for example, 'this box is a car,' or, 'these corks are chips'.
- Promote road safety consciousness through imaginative play on marked road systems, crossings, etc, where children use wheeled vehicles.

POINTS ALWAYS TO BE KEPT IN MIND

Do we provide sufficient space, time and freedom to encourage the children's creative abilities?

Are tools, props and materials available in sufficient quantity and quality?

Do we encourage:

> Improvisation?
>
> Experimentation?
>
> Problem solving?
>
> Abstract thinking?

Are we available for:

> Discussion?
>
> Social interaction?
>
> Sharing in the 'pretence'?
>
> Encouraging the completion of a task?
>
> Helping negotiations?
>
> Demonstrating a positive attitude towards the children's creations?

'Do we provide sufficient space, time and freedom to encourage the children's abilities?'

When it comes to stimulating the children's imaginations, do we:

- Offer a rich variety of stories or poems?
- Provide a wide variety of artistic examples on display?
- Present music from different cultures, remembering to balance modern and traditional styles?
- Sometimes play appropriate background music to support imaginative play?
- Recognise the importance of talk in inspiring children's imagination and sustaining it?
- Extend imaginative play into the outside area by painting marks onto the concrete or tarmac – for example 'footsteps' of giants, dragons, birds, dinosaurs which can inspire many children's games.

MUSIC MAKING

The enjoyment of music is an important part of human experience. We learn to be affected by it and to express ourselves through it.

However, it would be a shame if, through lack of self-confidence, adults failed to cater for children's needs. We cannot know all the ways in which children will be affected by music and can only witness their responses. They need to be able to both listen and to perform.

Do you provide children with opportunities to:
- Sing in a variety of settings – perhaps alone but often in a group.
- Express rhythms through sounds produced by:
  The voice exploring its range of sounds.
  Parts of the body – hands, feet.
  The use of instruments (made and bought) to beat, to shake, scrape, ring, blow and pluck.
- Combine sound with mime and dance, choosing the most appropriate sounds for the action concerned.
- Experiment freely with sound making equipment.
- Play guessing games about the instruments played behind a screen.
- Play at echoing sounds – one child or an adult plays, the others repeat the pattern of sound.
- Play a 'Pass the instrument' game – play when the music stops.

Can the children distinguish between:
  Loud/soft sounds.
  High/low sounds.
  Fast/slow rhythms.

Make up patterns of sound to match situations, eg a bird singing in a tree, an elephant walking, a rainy day.

Hold a 'sound conversation' in which children take it in turns to 'speak' using their instruments.

Keep the following instruments in your musical resources: Drum, tambourines, castanets, maracas, bells, triangles, claves, chime bars, recorders, pan pipes, xylophone, guitar or other stringed instruments.

CHAPTER 7

Planning a curriculum

The curriculum can be defined as all that occurs, both planned and unplanned, in a nursery setting – it is how, when and with whom the child experiences situations.

Why should we be planning a curriculum for under fives? It is important that these experiences should be wide and varied, as well as appropriate to the children's needs, to enable optimum development. If we do not match the experiences given by the curriculum to children's needs, we are doing them a disservice and failing in our role as educators.

'Understand the children's levels of development and then to plan a coherent set of experiences to meet them.'

To be able to do this, it is first necessary to understand the children's levels of development and then to plan a coherent set of experiences to meet them. To assess whether you are achieving this, you need to evaluate the outcome of your planning, which can be represented by Diagram 1 below.

What is a curriculum for the under fives?

- It is not the national curriculum, although aspects of this will be covered.
- It is not totally free play.
- It is a compromise between the two of the above, but is an entity in itself which recognises the unique nature of a child and also acknowledges that developmental stages are allied to certain boundaries and expectations.

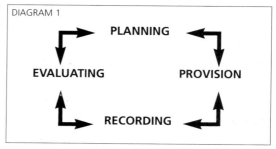

DIAGRAM 1

PLANNING

EVALUATING

PROVISION

RECORDING

To construct an appropriate curriculum, one must be aware of the social, emotional, physical and intellectual development of the child and consider the concepts, skills and attitudes that society expects the child to learn within the context of the environment (Diagram 2).

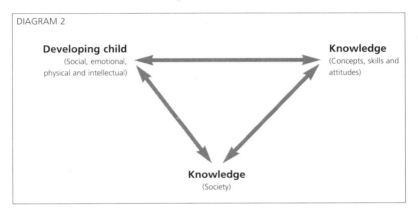

DIAGRAM 2

Developing child
(Social, emotional, physical and intellectual)

Knowledge
(Concepts, skills and attitudes)

Knowledge
(Society)

Knowledge can be further divided into areas of learning and this is where we begin to see a link with the national curriculum, as the children need a broad range of experiences to provide the foundations upon which further learning can be built.

How and what should we be planning?

It is necessary to plan as a team to provide a coherent presentation for the children, starting with a discussion and pooling of ideas. From this can come specific themes or foci that can be presented through various experiences.

It is important that the early years curriculum is seen as part of a continuum between, and complementary to, home and school activities. So, in any planning, one must take these points into consideration. Here is a model 'brainstorm' of how you might begin to plan around the central topic of 'Ourselves' (Diagram 3).

'It is necessary to plan as a team to provide a coherent presentation for the children, starting with a discussion and pooling of ideas.'

To develop one theme

The theme of taste, for example, can be presented through:

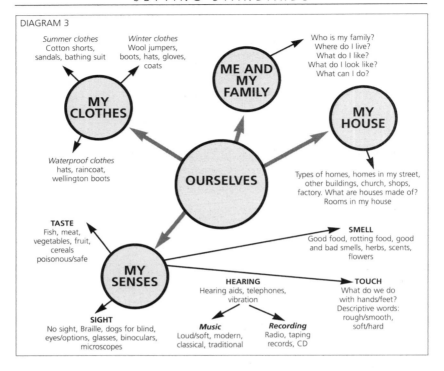

DIAGRAM 3

Summer clothes
Cotton shorts,
sandals, bathing suit

Winter clothes
Wool jumpers,
boots, hats, gloves,
coats

Who is my family?
Where do I live?
What do I like?
What do I look like?
What can I do?

ME AND MY FAMILY

MY CLOTHES

MY HOUSE

Waterproof clothes
hats, raincoat,
wellington boots

OURSELVES

Types of homes, homes in my street,
other buildings, church, shops,
factory. What are houses made of?
Rooms in my house

TASTE
Fish, meat,
vegetables, fruit,
cereals
poisonous/safe

SMELL
Good food, rotting food, good
and bad smells, herbs, scents,
flowers

MY SENSES

HEARING
Hearing aids, telephones,
vibration

TOUCH
What do we do
with hands/feet?
Descriptive words:
rough/smooth,
soft/hard

SIGHT
No sight, Braille, dogs for blind,
eyes/options, glasses, binoculars,
microscopes

Music
Loud/soft, modern,
classical, traditional

Recording
Radio, taping
records, CD

The home corner:	Looking at different shops/supermarket.
	Vegetables.
	Meat and Fish.
Water tray:	Foods dissolving.
	Pouring liquids.
Construction:	Large and small.
	Lego.
	Natural materials.
	Design and building shops.
	Making a 3D model of a shopping street.
Art:	Paint from the 'real' thing.
	Printing with food.
	Collages with food (melon pips).

Music: Songs about food.

Instruments made with dried fruits.

Book corner: books on shopping.

Where do different foods come from?

Which are good for us?

Sand tray: Moulding with different containers.

Cooking: Cooking various foods and recipes.

Food from other countries or cultures.

Dough: making food for the shop.

Writing: Shopping lists in the home corner.

Recipe books.

Maths: Money and till in the shop.

Sharing.

Display: Actual foods.

Science: Allows food to go 'off'.

Cut fruit and vegetables to examine.

'Are you planning for: the individual/ individuals within a small group/whole groups?'

Questions to ask when planning

Are you planning for: the individual/individuals within a small group/whole groups?

- What are the previous experiences of the children and what are your expectations?
- How long are you planning for: one week, one month, longer?
- Will you involve others in your planning?
- Who will record the plans?
- How do you decide the topic to brainstorm?

Consider: The time of year, children's needs/interests, special events, the immediate environment, natural phenomena, literature.

- How wide-ranging is this brainstorm? Which themes do you find most useful?
- In which order should they be presented, and what is the timetable for their presentation?

- Do the themes allow for a balanced curriculum, ie are you providing experiences for the children that reflect the different areas of learning?
- Are you also able to identify the concepts, skills and attitudes that the children may learn from these themes?
- What activities lend themselves to presenting these themes: sand, water, home corner, music?
- Will you need to alter the layout of the room?
- How should staff, children and parents be involved?
- Determine the resources you will need.
- Will staff need to 'top up' their knowledge?

'Planning does not end with the presentation of the experiences to the children.'

Planning does not end with the presentation of the experiences to the children – afterwards it is necessary to record the outcomes and evaluate how effective and worthwhile the experiences have been.

Below is a detailed examination of one area of learning – mathematics – which is part of everyday life. Shopping, cooking, making and mending, keeping things in order, pouring the tea and laying the table are all mathematical experiences. In so far as the nursery reflects everyday life (and it does) then we have ample opportunities to exploit the mathematical potential of children's play and experience.

Look at your setting – what mathematical experiences are you already providing in addition to the above examples? List any other experiences you could be providing. Take each experience in turn and identify the concepts that can be presented to the children through play. There will be opportunities to develop more than one concept in each experience. Having listed the concepts, can you identify the progression within each?

Can you map the experience to the concept, then to the progression, using the following model as one example?

EXPERIENCE–CONCEPT–PROGRESSION

Using the theme of 'The Three Bears' we take laying the table for the bears' breakfast.

One-to-one correspondence: Cardinal numbers (counting): 1,2,3.

Ordinal numbers: first, second, third.

Measurement: Matching size of object to size of bear:

small, smaller than, smallest, middle sized.

Temperature: hot/cold; hot,hotter, hottest

cold,colder, coldest.

Sets: Sorting according to child's own criteria – cutlery, dishes, and so on.

Sequencing and pattern: The order of items on the table.

other possible orders.

Volume: Full/empty.

Full, fuller, fullest.

More than/less than.

Most/least.

How many bowls can be filled from the amount in the porridge saucepan?

When observing children's play, can you use your detailed mapping to improve the quality of the intervention, thus enhancing the children's learning? And consider: are your resources matched to the task?

'Consider: are your resources matched to the task?'

Other points not to be missed

- Are you all, as a group, presenting a positive attitude to maths?
- Do the displays reflect children's mathematical learning?
- Are some displays capable of inspiring curiosity and investigation?
- Have you considered the mathematical potential of the outside environment?
- Have you made sure that parent helpers as well as the whole team are aware of the link between activity and language if mathematical concepts are to be acquired?

- If you have a computer, how is it being used?
- What areas of mathematical activity should children be undertaking?
- Counting.
- Matching.
- Enjoying related songs and rhymes.
- Measuring – capacity, time, length, height, temperature, weight.
- Sorting and matching – encourages the ability to classify and compare.
- Construction – involving a variety of materials and equipment.
- Pattern and sequencing.
- Shape – 2D and 3D.
- Scale – 'small world' work helps develop the understanding of this. Children should be encouraged to estimate even at this early stage, eg: 'How many dollies' cups do you think we can fill from the teapot?'

CHAPTER 8

Behaviour and discipline

When talking about 'bad' behaviour we must remember that young children in a nursery are still very egocentric and that much of what society deems desirable – politeness, honesty, consideration for others etc – has to be learned.

Bad behaviour almost invariably occurs when children's fundamental needs are frustrated. It is important, therefore, for adults to consider what their needs are and how we can best meet them. As well as the obvious need for sustenance and shelter, children must be provided with:

'Bad behaviour almost invariably occurs when children's fundamental needs are frustrated.'

- Love and care.
- Security.
- Adequate rest and sleep.
- Freedom to explore, within their physical capability and the limits of safety.
- Adults who will encourage the development of a positive self-image.
- Adults who will act as appropriate role models.
- Consistency in treatment.
- Boundaries or limits to behaviour.
- Opportunities for self-expression.
- Opportunities for learning.

The onus is on the adults to respect children and to determine the rules to enable children to flourish. There are many factors in today's society, perceived or real, which lead to the popular view that children's behaviour is deteriorating. Those working with them must accept the responsibility of promoting 'good' behaviour, the broad ideas of which are shared by all cultures.

1. Love and care

How do we show children that we love and care for them?

At what times will they most particularly need to feel loved?

Do we provide equally for all children overcoming any tendency to favouritism?

Do we honestly hear what the children are saying?

Does all our non-verbal communication reinforce what we are saying?

'Do we provide equally for all children overcoming any tendency to favouritism?'

2. Security

Does the way we structure our daily or weekly programme foster a feeling of security?

In our organisation – do children know when things happen? Where things are? Where particular people are to be found?

Do we warn them of impending change?

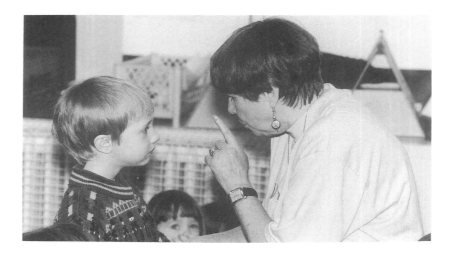

3. Adequate rest and sleep

Are there places where children can withdraw quietly for time out – a comfortable chair, cushions, bean bags, bed, lap or quiet corner – both inside and outside?

Are children able to have a 'comforter' with them? A blanket, toy, familiar object, book, music?

Can we provide as much time as they need to rest?

Are we liaising with parents on this issue?

4. Freedom to explore

Is there the space for children to 'let off steam'? If not, what alternatives can we offer?

Do we change the environment so that it is worth exploring?

How do we determine the balance between free and adult-directed activity for individual children?

Analyse the possibilities for exploration within your setting. How varied are they?

'Analyse the possibilities for exploration within your setting.'

5. The importance of self image

A child with a poor self-image is unlikely to behave well.

How do we promote a good self-image among our children?

Do we praise whenever we can?

Do we give individuals time and attention?

Do we value all their tangible contributions, including things brought from home – drawings etc?

Do we give children opportunities to 'shine'?

Do the children see that we like their families?

6. Adults as role models

Examine such questions as:

dress

manner of speaking

body language

tolerance

politeness and consideration

the value of humour

hygiene.

7. **Consistency in treatment**

Is it obvious to the children that we are fair in sharing access to toys?

Does the same behaviour elicit the same treatment whether it concerns individuals or a group?

Are the rewards we give consistently fair, ie praise or favours and privileges?

8. **Boundaries to behaviour**

Do both adults and children fully understand what is expected of them and each other?

Are expectations realistic? If they are not, bad behaviour is likely to ensue.

Do we modify our expectations in the light of a child's level of maturity and ability?

Are we fair and consistent when called upon to arbitrate?

How do we register approval and disapproval of actions?

Do we always remember the importance of highlighting the action and not the child?

Do we regularly remind children of the expectations we have established and offer explanations for them?

9. **Opportunities for self-expression**

Do the children feel free to say what they want to say?

Are they free to express their opinions and needs through actions and artistic activities?

Do we enable children to work through traumatic experiences through such acceptable means as drama, role play, artistic and physical expression? The way a child treats his toy may be an indicator of the child's state of mind and/or experiences.

Is it appropriate for children to curtail their self-expression in certain circumstances?

What about the withdrawn child – how do we encourage him to express himself?

'There are many factors at home and in society which may adversely affect children's behaviour.'

10. Opportunities for learning

Busy, involved and happy children engaged in appropriate tasks are much less likely to be disruptive.

Factors beyond the nursery which affect children's behaviour

There are many factors at home and in society which may adversely affect children's behaviour. Some of these are within a worker's power to influence, while others cannot be realistically changed.

It is important to recognise these factors but not allow them to predetermine expectations of a child.

List adverse factors that might affect the children and identify those you might be able to modify and how you would set about doing so.

AN EXAMPLE OF LACK OF ROUTINE AT HOME:

Ms A lives in a state of loving chaos – she frequently comes in late. Her timetable is chaotic. The child begins the session tired. Meal times and bed times are very erratic. The house is open to all the neighbours who take advantage of her good nature. Tom fends largely for himself, much of his time is spent in unrestricted television viewing. In the group he presents as a boy who lacks concentration, clings to the adults and is reluctant to play with others. In outside play he is sometimes rough. What could you do?

Discipline and sanctions

What if the child does transgress despite all your best efforts? Adults have a responsibility to themselves, the children and society to say 'no' sometimes. Can you avert unacceptable behaviour by diverting the child's attention or through the use of kindly humour?

How and when is the 'no' to be said?

Is there a 'warning' procedure?

What happens when the warnings have run out?

Could the child be removed from the scene for a time?

'Adults have a responsibility to themselves, the children and society to say 'no' sometimes.'

What about giving a stern reprimand – how should your voice sound?

Should the reprimand be in private?

How do we convey that the deed has been forgiven and fresh start established?

Remember that we need to 'build a warm bridge' again as soon as possible and avoid labelling or stereotyping the child 'naughty'.

Conflict should never linger.

Should we deny privileges and opportunities?

How and when should parents become involved?

Any child presenting difficult behaviour on a regular basis should become a subject for close observation. Identify:

- The nature of the behaviour
- Factors or circumstances which trigger it.
- Timings – when, how long for?
- People involved.
- How does it end?

The observations need to be written and examined for identifiable patterns and then decisions made about future handling. Such observations provide objective evidence in discussion with parents or other professionals.

CHAPTER 9

Every child an individual

Early years workers have an essential role to play in developing each child's self-confidence; even more so when children are under stress at home or when their home environment does little to promote their sense of self-worth.

We can only know the needs of individual children entering our establishment through building up a detailed profile of them on entry and continuing to update it for as long as they remain with us. We need to first draw upon the intimate knowledge possessed by the child's parents or carers, and their observations should be included in the dynamic process of record keeping.

Parents will have become used to discussing their child's needs and progress with other professionals before they come to the nursery. Many health authorities have handed over ownership of children's medical records to parents, and, in so doing, have begun to break down negative feelings about the medical profession's mystique and power.

'It is important that a working knowledge of child development should underpin practice.'

All children develop along a determined continuum but at different rates. A good under fives setting must cater for the social, emotional, physical and intellectual components of this continuum. It is important, therefore, that a working knowledge of child development should underpin practice and staff must never lose sight of this.

Added to this are the group contexts to which the child belongs – gender, race, nationality and culture. An individual's positive self-image can only be achieved through a policy of equal opportunities that sets out to eliminate all negative discrimination. Indeed, an important part of the work of any nursery is to actively promote a sense of self-worth among its children. For many, this will complement the love and encouragement received at home. For less fortunate children, however, from all strata of society, it is incumbent upon staff to attempt to heal the emotional damage done through negative treatment and compensate through care, encouragement and attention as well as working, wherever possible, with the parents and carers concerned.

We are all aware of the increasing strain in many family relationships which must be attributed, at least in part, to difficult economic circumstances. Parental disputes, for whatever reason, lead to feelings of insecurity among children, as do other family traumas like bereavement or illness.

'Parental disputes, for whatever reason, lead to feelings of insecurity among children, as do other family traumas like bereavement or illness.'

FAMILY BREAKDOWN

Research from the 'National Child Development Study' (1991) reveals the severely traumatic effect of family breakdown. Manifestations of this include the emotional problems experienced by children:

- Prior to divorce.
- During the process of divorce and separation.
- During the forging of the step-family.
- And by the child or children of the young single parent who may have left their own parental home through unhappiness there.

Staff need to be particularly sensitive towards these children where suffering may be going unnoticed.

Disrupted families frequently experience difficulties and staff should be aware of this pressure, which can manifest itself in:

- The inability to provide an adequate nutritional diet.
- Inability to contribute to nursery funds.
- Inability to clothe children adequately.

Staff may be able to direct parents to agencies offering advice on benefits, etc.

Our work, then, in developing the confidence of all children, is not only important for the here and now – as confident children are likely to be happier in their relationships with peers and adults alike – but it also enhances the likelihood of their becoming competent and fulfilled adults.

Adults show by their very demeanour that they find children's company pleasurable. Appropriate cuddles, smiles and pleasant manner of speaking generate an atmosphere of encouragement. Adults should readily engage in children's play or invite children into theirs. Children are sensitive to the moods and feelings of individuals, and adults should help them to come to terms with the natural anger and frustration which is part of childhood.

Adults should take time to give eye contact to children and listen to them when they speak. Children should be encouraged to initiate their own activities, and make their own choices.

Successes should be celebrated and failures or mistakes treated in a positive light.

'Children are sensitive to the moods and feelings of individuals, and adults should help them to come to terms with the natural anger and frustration which is part of childhood.'

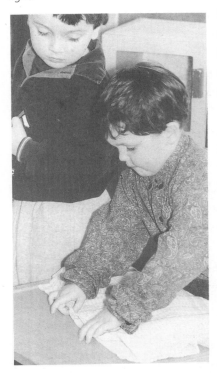

Children should be given responsibilities appropriate to their individual stage of development. The accomplishment of these is then an occasion for praise.

RESOURCES

Resources reflect our belief in gender equality.

You need to avoid books, pictures, puzzles and toys that perpetuate male/female stereotypical roles. You need to have an equal number of male/female dolls and the settings, props and clothes provided for role play should be equally accessed by boys and girls; significant examples being bikes, prams, dolls, woodwork, home corner, cooking, large blocks, cars and trucks.

Appropriate resources should be available to children in order to encourage independence and choice. There are ample 'small world' games which enable children to 'govern' an imagined situation.

THE ROLE MODELS WE PROVIDE PROMOTE EQUAL OPPORTUNITIES

- Encourage fathers and grandfathers to help as well as mothers and grandmothers.
- Invite both male and female visitors.
- Invite people who are generally not well represented in a particular role, for example, a lady doctor or a father bathing a baby.
- Organise group activities which avoid dividing the children by gender, for example, 'girls line up first', 'let the girls clear up', 'we need strong boys to move the furniture'.
- Be careful to avoid statements like 'two quiet girls', 'three strong boys', 'boys don't cry' and 'little girls don't fight'.
- Represent different cultures in your resources.
- Demonstrate a positive attitude to different races and cultures at discussion times.

- Encourage people from different ethnic backgrounds to become involved in the work of the nursery.
- Emphasise the value of cultural diversity through learning about different festivals and celebrations.
- Provide dressing-up clothes to include costumes worn by different ethnic groups.
- Cook recipes from around the world with cooking utensils as varied as the recipes.
- Collect artifacts and resources from a variety of cultures – use them for display and to stimulate children's interest.
- The range of paint provided enables children to approximate their skin tones.
- Have a welcome notice in different languages and display different scripts and dual-text books.
- Respect restrictions and religious injunctions and practices.
- Where possible, take children to shops where goods pertaining to different cultures are on display.
- Take special care to avoid negative national and cultural stereotypes of all kinds developing in the minds of young children; these have no place in the wider community to which we all belong.

'The range of paint provided enables children to approximate their skin tones.'

CHAPTER 10

The special needs of gifted children

Early years workers may be the first to spot a child's special needs – whether they have arisen due to late development, a handicap, or an above-average ability.

Statistically, all groups will have a number of children who present with some identifiable special need which may either remain with them throughout life (eg cerebral palsy) or be of a temporary nature, such as 'lazy eye', 'glue ear' or speech problems.

Some children will come to us precisely because they have a specific identified need, for others the need will become apparent as they develop within the group. In the latter case, parents may suspect that a problem exists and discuss it with us. Our own observations may or may not confirm their fears.

A more difficult scenario can occur when we become concerned with an aspect of a child's development and must then sensitively draw the parents' attention to this, supporting them in seeking professional advice where necessary.

Children with special needs may fall into one or more of these broad categories:

Physical disability.

Sensory impairment.

Speech and language problems.

Learning difficulties.

Emotional/behaviour problems.

Possible abuse.

Gifted children.

In the scope of this chapter, it is impossible to go into detail about every special need so we concentrate on gifted children, but we offer a list of questions which could be applied to most cases to help you identify and cater for the individual.

What do you know about the child?

- How can you extend your knowledge of the child?

    Ask parents.

    Ask other professionals.

    Systematically observe the child.

- What do you know about the child's need? How could you extend this knowledge? By consulting:

    Parents.

    Other professionals.

    Local support groups.

    National societies.

    Books/pamphlets.

- Does the child need:

    Physical aids.

    Special diet.

    Special facilities.

    Individual attention

    from an assigned worker.

    Particular toys/equipment.

    Regular medication.

    Special transport.

    Special learning programme.

    Peripatetic support?

Can you meet the identified needs?

If you cannot, you should be asking yourself if the child would be more appropriately placed elsewhere.

If the child is to remain with you then you must address these points:

'How do you
intend to
monitor the
child's
development
and progress
in the nursery.'

- Staff may need in-service training.
- The child's membership of groups and access to activities must be carefully planned.
- The understanding and support of the parents may also need to be enlisted.
- Will you need to modify the curriculum?
- How do you intend to monitor the child's development and progress in the nursery?
- How will you work with the child's parents to maximise his development?
- Careful consideration must be given to the child's next placement and good liaison established.

What about the gifted child?

A gifted child has special needs. You and the child's parents will have to work closely together both to identify and meet these needs. First, one has to distinguish between children who demonstrate a gift in a particular field – eg maths, music, art or sport – and those who are gifted with an all-round high intelligence.

The former are often to be found in a household where the culture is very much centred around a particular activity; thus from an early age the child is steeped in an environment which encourages his or her participation. The child gifted with a high IQ, however, can be born into just about any household.

How can adults be helped to identify such a child, and how can they help nurture giftedness? Some pointers in identifying gifted children are:

- Gifted children have an intense curiosity about the world around them and ask frequent, searching questions.
- They demonstrate an early ability to reason.
- They are interested in cause and effect.
- They are capable of sustained concentration on tasks which interest them.
- They display a great need to be active and involved and generally require much less sleep than other children their own age.
- They have excellent memories.
- They often learn to read without any apparent effort being made to teach them.
- They are frequently intrigued by numbers and the patterning inherent in mathematics and music.

Nurturing giftedness

Such children need plenty of access to adult time to pose their questions, engage in conversation and enjoy sharing their enthusiasm for finding out about things, performing, etc.

If you are privileged enough to be educating a gifted child do you:

- Help to find answers to questions through encouraging observation, experimentation, asking those who know?
- Avoid going beyond the child's capacity to attend?
- Avoid concentrating exclusively on the intellectual dimension of the child's development at the expense of the rest?
- Avoid a pedantic insistence on accuracy to the exclusion of the joy inherent in the activity?
- Provide opportunities for recording information to support the child's enthusiasm – through scrap books, drawings, diagrams, etc?
- Encourage adults to make some time available to the child?

- Make available examples of works produced by adults gifted in the field in question?
- Make sure that such children feel loved for what they are, not for what they can do?

CHAPTER 11

Observation and record keeping

Observing children in our care and keeping good records is the shared responsibility of nursery workers.

Why should we observe children and keep records on them?

To come up with a satisfactory answer to this question we need to ask 'What are we observing?' and 'What are we observing for?'

Observation is a useful tool to enable us to assess:

Individual development.

Behaviour.

Use of resources.

Co-operation.

Social interaction.

Policies on areas such as special educational needs.

Equal opportunities.

Observation is a responsibility of every team member through:

(a) A planned, regular programme.

(b) Noting significant occurrences.

Every child is entitled to his share of focused adult attention through a rolling programme of regular, detailed observation. If this is not carried out, certain children, by their very nature, demand more than their fair share of adult time while others, of a quieter nature whose needs are just as great, may go unnoticed.

Observation enables us to determine a child's stage of development and provide for future needs. It also helps us to identify children with special needs.

Observations may also contain objective information that may be shared with colleagues and parents.

Ask yourself:
- Can students/parents help in the observation programme?
- Where do you place yourself to observe?
  (a) as a fly on the wall?
  (b) fully participating in the children's activity?
- What is the effect on children of knowing that they are being observed? Could this influence the validity of the observation?
- Should we 'set up' a situation to enable us to look for particular attainments?

'Should we 'set up' a situation to enable us to look for particular attainments?'

How do we record our observations?
- In a notebook?
- With a tape recorder?
- With a video recorder?
- Using tangible children's work?
- Making use of pre-determined headings on a record sheet?

How do we edit our observations? And having edited them what do they tell us?
If we have insufficient information should we re-examine the child?
How far should we include the observations of parents and other professionals?
Do we observe with the format of a pre-determined record sheet in mind or create a record sheet from our observations?

What of the child with special needs?
- Do we use the same strategies?
- Do we devise different strategies?
- Do we need to observe the child more or less frequently?

- If we use a pre-determined record, do we need to break down areas of achievement more finely?
- Should we concentrate on specific areas of development depending on the child's needs?
- Are our observations being used by other professionals; if so, how might this affect the way we complete them?
- If we are working with other professionals are we agreed about what we are looking for?

Observation is recording what is being done and what is said. It is not to be distorted or altered by interpretation and care has to be taken here.

The need to be objective

Inevitably, observers bring their own ideas and experiences to the task, which can distort the observation. Great care has to be taken to be objective: accent, dress, haircut, an earring, or a swear word are capable of distorting our view of a child and this distortion could interfere with the observation. Such bias could include having an individual child as a favourite, or disliking another, and seeing their behaviour in 'positive' or 'negative' terms. Knowing parents and a child's background can also interfere with the observation.

The need to avoid interpretation

We must not interpret at the same time as we observe.

Positive interpretation:
- He did that *because* he was disturbed.
- He can really do that but...
- He would have done it if...

Negative interpretation:
- It was because... helped him.
- He must have copied.
- He must have had a sudden burst of inspiration.

The setting

Make the conditions suitable for the observation as objective as possible. The day must be 'normal' and there should be as few disruptions as possible. The time when the observation takes place needs to be as normal as possible too – avoiding occasions when the child is 'off colour' or upset. Be practical; observation is time consuming – but not more than ten minutes can be spent on a given child.

If we observe children we can really speak authoritatively about them. Haphazard observations tend to concentrate on the 'naughty', the 'charismatic', or the child with special needs – and in this way some children are occasionally ignored. Observation is essential to provide appropriately for the child and inform parents of their child's development.

Good record keeping enables us to:

- Assess what the child has learned and the stage of development reached.
- Ascertain readiness for the next stage.
- Plan our programmes.
- Diagnose difficulties experienced by individuals with a view to helping them.
- Identify special needs, including those of the very able.
- Communicate more effectively with:
  (a) Members of our team.
  (b) Parents/carers.
  (c) Teachers.
  (d) Other agencies including playgroups, health visitors, schools.

What should be included in a child's record?

A baseline should be formed:

- As a result of home visits/discussion with parents.
- Through observations from other agencies, eg health clinic or playgroup.

The observations should be organised into:

Basic factual information:

- Name, date of birth, address, mother tongue, religion etc.

Development areas:

- Social/emotional.
- Language and literacy.
- Aesthetic/creative/imaginative.
- Physical – fine motor/gross motor.
- Technological/problem solving.
- Scientific.
- Mathematical.

The observations should be:

(a) Regular, to show progress.

(b) Systematic.

(c) Objective – what is said and done as opposed to assertions.

(d) Dated.

Tangible examples of children's work – emergent writing/drawings, paintings, as well as tape recording should be included.

Any incoming information about circumstances at home or in the group which may influence the present position should be included in the record and dated. Projects which the child has shared in should be noted.

What should records be based upon?

The detailed observations of those who care for and work with the child. Clearly, parents know their children better than anyone else and their contribution to the records is to be welcomed both on entry to the group and as a continuing process.

Other agencies will have made observations of the child, and their contributions should form part of his or her profile through fully understood and agreed practices. These include the social worker, day nursery officer-in-charge, childminder, parent and toddler group, playgroup, teacher, nursery nurse, general practitioner, health visitor, speech therapist and psychologist.

It's important that a means of communication is set up to facilitate this, possibly through local under fives groups. Staff should make every effort to liaise with the receiver of the records.

Points to consider

- Avoid formal testing as opposed to observing the child engaged naturally in activities planned for or allowed by the staff.
- Play will be the context for almost all the child's learning and development at this stage.
- Set up a regular and uninterrupted observation programme.
- It is valuable to keep a notebook and pen 'in the pocket' for significant observations which occur outside the programme.
- In company with colleagues and partners, evolve a system which is right for your situation. If it is agreed, workable, informative and useful, then you will have done a good job.
- Records will be kept on children who should pursue a curriculum which is broad, balanced and planned to ensure continuity and progression, and rooted in purposeful play. It should be enjoyable, promote thinking and problem solving, improve language competence, and encourage the exploration and investigation of materials including experimentation.
- Staff need to use their records to make sure that this experience of the curriculum is happening for all children; note therefore needs to be taken of what is not said as well as what is said.
- Some children will be achieving in areas of the national curriculum, so staff need to acquaint themselves with all NC documents as they are part of the educational continuum along which all children will progress.
- The need to plan 'next stages' must be rooted in a knowledge of individual children's previous experience, competence and understanding.
- Try to avoid over attention to detail or saying too little to be helpful.
- Staff should meet regularly to discuss records.

- Emphasis should be on what children can do.
- Should children contribute to their own records?
- New ideas, research findings and social changes mean that records cannot be 'set in stone'. They need to be regularly evaluated and changed in the light of new needs and circumstances.

Here are a possible three ways of organising record keeping

1. The whole staff target a group of children who will be carefully observed over a week. It is helpful to be able to identify these children through letting them wear a 'smiley' badge or something similar. The staff will then meet at the end of the week to pool their observations. The advantage of this system is that it enables the child to be seen in a variety of settings and with a variety of people. In this way, observer bias may be minimised.

2. Individual members of staff target given children for uninterrupted observation during a five to ten minute period. To ensure all children are given equal attention these observations need to be undertaken on a rotational basis.

3. Staff need to carry a notebook and pen so they can record significant developments while participating in children's activities. These notes can be added to a child's records at a convenient time.

CHAPTER 12

The case for learning through play

With the advent of the national curriculum, and its concomitant statutory and regular assessment procedures, parents have become very anxious about the success of their children at each stage in their schooling. This has prompted them to believe that unless their children's early education is formalised, they may be disadvantaged when meeting the assessment at seven years old.

Local management of schools has also put pressure on governing bodies to accept 'rising fives' as a way of guaranteeing pupil numbers in the future. The settings they are able to provide are often inadequately funded and have inappropriate resources.

For these reasons, nursery staff may well find themselves in the position of having to justify and educate others as to the value of children's play as a necessary learning medium in early childhood education. It is imperative that those professionals working with young children should be able to articulate clearly and with confidence the value and place of play in a child's social, emotional, physical and intellectual development, presenting each of these aspects as being of equal importance.

For a child there is no distinction between work and play. The innate predisposition to play occurs at a time of most rapid intellectual growth prompted by an intense curiosity about themselves, the world around them and social relationships.

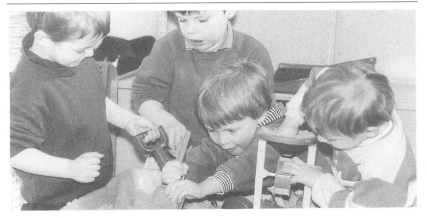

EXTENDING PLAY

A feature which must distinguish us as professionals in childcare and education, is our ability to know when and how to extend children's learning through play. We do this by observing either as participants or by standing back and taking note of what is said and done. We cannot go forward without knowing exactly where our starting point is! But what do we really mean by 'extending children's play', and how can we create a manageable framework in which to do this? Breaking the task down into units is probably the best way to achieve our aims. The following format will prove helpful.

Analyse the current situation and ask yourselves how you can extend the range of opportunities through:

- Use of language.
- Range of materials.
- Range of skills.
- Different social contacts.
- Different experiences both in and out of the nursery.

Knowledgeable and observant staff will be able to identify the following types of play occurring in their nursery, and will be able to use actual situations to enable them to give illustrations of each type when they are talking about the place of play in a child's early education.

'A feature which must distinguish us as professionals in childcare and education, is our ability to know when and how to extend children's learning through play.'

EXPLORATORY PLAY

This is the first aspect of play to emerge in a young child, and can be seen in babies as young as three months, continuing throughout life. Through exploratory play children learn about:

- Their body – what it can and cannot do, what it looks and feels like, how to control it, and how the body's senses receive information from the surrounding environment.
- The nature of materials and their various properties such as texture, colour, weight and malleability.
- Physical laws, for example looking at gravity, force and acoustics.
  Such learning is obviously enhanced when it is accompanied by the attention of an adult who is happy to discuss these topics with the children.

SYMBOLIC PLAY

This involves the child in appreciating and agreeing that some things can stand for others. In the earliest stages a doll will stand for a baby, a hand-held animal model will stand for the real thing. A more abstract form of symbolic play will occur when, for example, a toilet roll tube becomes a pirate's telescope. An appreciation that such objects represent others will enable the child to accept, at a later stage, that words and numbers stand for objects and ideas which are not actually present.

'A more abstract form of symbolic play will occur when, for example, a toilet roll tube becomes a pirate's telescope.'

PHYSICAL PLAY

It would be true to say that the medical profession is concerned about the long-term implications of the present-day lifestyle of children. Muscle tone and circulatory and respiratory systems are often not sufficiently exercised for healthy development. The old adage 'a healthy mind in a healthy body' is as true today as it was in ancient Rome. We cannot disassociate other aspects of human development from the physical, and the following points should help to make this clear.

The exploration of space through running, jumping, swinging, climbing, hanging upside down, twisting, turning and rolling activities that children enjoy, gives them many of the experiences they need before they can understand the spatial aspects of mathematics, physics, engineering and technology.

Moreover, pushing and pulling wheeled vehicles in the nursery garden teaches them about physical forces. They will also learn how to judge speed and distance, and how to manoeuvre more safely in an outdoor environment. Physical play can also provide them with much-needed challenge and adventure in a safe environment.

Much of their physical play will involve hand-to-eye co-ordination, as in playing with balls, hoops, bean-bags, and so on. Sometimes equipment must be shared, so the social lessons of taking turns and being first, even last to use items has to be understood, as well as the need for rules if games are to have a happy and successful outcome.

When staff structure music, movement and drama sessions, children must learn to listen in order to respond appropriately. This will help develop language, as well as giving staff the opportunity to assess understanding. Children will learn about what their bodies can do. It will also give them important aesthetic experiences, for example, the joy of dancing and responding to rhythm. Dance is, after all, a fundamental and universal means of expression.

'The social lessons of taking turns and being first, even last to use items has to be understood.'

Fine motor skills entail hand-to-eye co-ordination such as threading, using tools for writing, art and craft, the manipulation of equipment such as Lego and jigsaw puzzles, then learning all the self-help skills involved in dressing themselves or dressing dolls. The development of such skills promotes competence in so many facets of practical life.

Role play

This is important in enabling children to practise behaviour in different social settings and to begin to understand how people relate to one another. They can experiment with roles of leadership and compliance, and thus learn the appropriate ways of acting and reacting in different situations. It also encourages

them to empathise, and to use language both in spoken and 'written'* forms appropriate to the setting. For some children role play has a cathartic value, in that fears or worries can be played out and resolved in a safe environment. This becomes increasingly necessary as children come to terms with the harsh realities of everyday life in the twentieth century, often relayed to them via the media.
(* 'Written' here means emergent writing.)

Creative play

This occurs as a child identifies the need to make or represent something, choosing from a variety of media. We need to help children acquire the skills and techniques for their ideas to come to fruition.

Through using play materials, children learn to care for group property and to be aware of the responsibility involved in careful storage and respecting other people's 'precious' things.

Imagination is a component of most play, its development is necessary for success in all areas of learning. Indeed, there is no situation or subject which, if to be successfully mastered, does not require the imaginative leap of discovery and understanding.

Finally, play is experimental, and does not demand a right or wrong outcome. Questions can be asked in a supportive, non-judgmental environment. Through this positive ethos children should be able to feel that they can do anything, be able to have a go at everything, thereby creating a positive self-image. Children will then be encouraged to make choices, exercise their judgement, achieve self-set goals and use skills learned to extend their knowledge of the world around them, and thus become independent and effective learners.

BLATCHFORD, P, BATTLE, S. and MAYS, J. (1982)
The First Transition Windsor, NFER – Nelson

BROWNE, N. and FRANCE, P. editors (1986)
Untying the Apron Strings, Milton Keynes – Open University Press

BRUCE, T. (1987)
Early Childhood Education, London – Hodder and Stoughton

Commission for Racial Equality (1989)
From Cradle to School, London – C.R.E.

CURTIS, A. (1986)
A Curriculum for the Pre–School Child, Windsor, NFER – Nelson

DEPARTMENT OF EDUCATION AND SCIENCE (1989)
The Education of Children Under Five, London – H.M.S.O.

Early Years Curriculum Group (1992)
First Things First, Pub. – E.Y.C.G.

GAMMAGE, P. and MEIGHAN, J, editors (1993)
Early Childhood Education: Taking Stock – Ticknall Education Now
Publishing Co-operative

HURST, V (1991)
Planning for Early Learning, London – Paul Chapman Publishing

LALLY, M (1991)
The Nursery Teacher in Action, London – Paul Chapman Publishing

MOYLES, J.R. (1989)
Just Playing? Milton Keynes – Open University Press

PUGH, G and DE'ATH, E (1989)
Working towards partnership in the early years – National Children's Bureau

Do you subscribe to

NURSERY?
WORLD

A six month subscription to Nursery World costs just £20, and you also receive a Nursery World binder (worth £8.99) to keep your issues in - completely free of charge!

Why _you_ should subscribe to Nursery World today.

- you will keep up-to-date with the latest news – such as the Government's plans for nursery vouchers

- you will receive the very best project ideas – including pull-out posters to use with the children you look after

- you will be able to enjoy regular features in areas such as child development and best practice in nurseries

- you will be the first to know about all the latest new jobs each week

Begin your subscription now. Simply complete the order form below or ring our Subscriptions Hotline on 0171-837 8515.

• ORDER FORM •

Please enter an introductory six-month subscription to Nursery World at a cost of only £20 for 25 weeks.

Please also send me a free binder worth £8.99.

☐ I enclose a cheque/PO for £20.

☐ I enclose a purchase order. Please send me an invoice.
(invoice not available for private individuals)

Your Name and Address

☐Miss ☐Ms ☐Mrs ☐Mr Name _____

Job Title _____

Establishment _____

Address _____

_____

Town _____ County _____ Postcode _____

Tel No. (in case of queries) _____

Credit Card Payments Only

Card Number _____   Expiry Date

☐☐☐☐☐☐☐☐☐☐☐☐☐☐☐☐   ☐☐ / ☐☐

☐ Miss ☐ Ms ☐Mrs ☐Mr Name _____

Address _____

_____

Town _____County _____ Postcode _____

Signed _____ **Date** _____

Credit Card Orders Hotline
Phone 0171-837 8515 and ask for Nursery World Subscriptions.

Our Address
Send this completed form together with your remittance or credit card details to Nursery World Ltd. to Nursery World, Freepost WD29, London WC1 0BR. No stamp is necessary in UK. Set Sub